Pattern
Fun

By Amy Houts

CELEBRATION PRESS
Pearson Learning Group

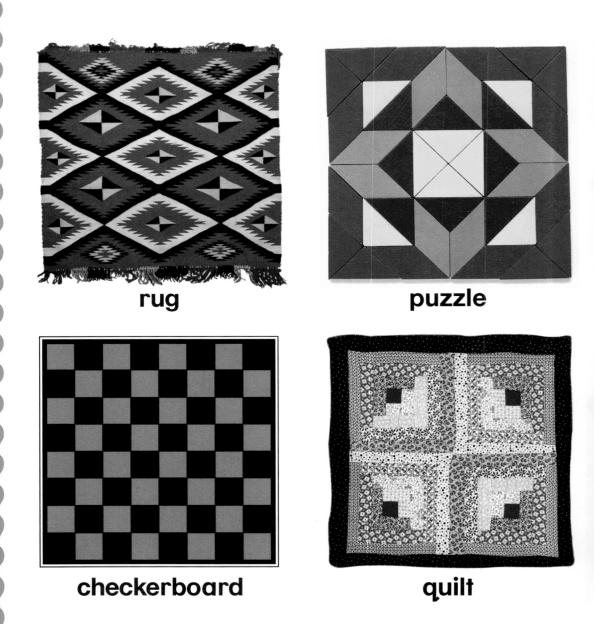

rug

puzzle

checkerboard

quilt

Patterns are shapes or colors that repeat.

You can make a pattern.
You can make a mat.

1 Cut strips of paper.

2 Fold a sheet of paper.

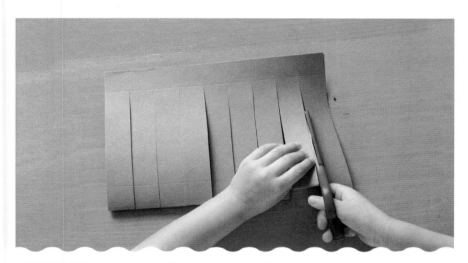

3 Cut lines that go near the edge.

4 Weave a strip of paper over and under.

5 Weave a new color strip under and over.

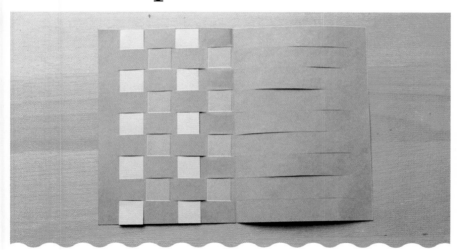

6 Repeat your pattern until you are finished.

Look. You made a pattern!